Poetry speaks truths
to the listening
Soul.

Love   A

Poetry by Michael Byrne
Estuary at Dusk
Southbound

On Common Water

Poems selected by

Michael Byrne

GINNINDERRA PRESS

On Common Water
ISBN 1 74027 362 1
Copyright © poems: individual authors 2006
Copyright © this collection: Michael Byrne 2006
Cover photo: Heide Seaman

This collection first published 2006 by
GINNINDERRA PRESS
PO Box 6753 Charnwood ACT 2615 Australia
www.ginninderrapress.com.au

Printed by Pirion Digital, Fyshwick, ACT

Contents

Introduction

I have tried to incorporate a variety of poetic styles in this anthology, which brings together the work of 50 poets published by Ginninderra Press and its sister imprint Indigo between 1996 and 2006.

There are sonnets, ballads, haiku, free-verse poems, poems without punctuation, and prose poems. The anthology incorporates other poetic styles too and also has a variety of subject matter: there are political poems, poems about people, poems about places, and dichotomies between the Antipodean and the wider world, as well as the urban and the rural.

There are certainly Australian themes here, which reflect my personal taste. Dogs, surfing, cakes, Australian Rules football, as well as places such as Hobart and Bali, have all found their way into the book.

But as much as this anthology is about me, it's also about everyone else who has been included.*

Michael Byme

* Publisher's note: Ginninderra Press has published the work of many more than 50 poets but, with the limited space available to us in this volume, only living poets resident in Australia whose books were listed in the current catalogue at the end of January 2006 were invited to have one of their poems included.

Sort of Kind of Like

Promiscuous as hair on the floor of the barber's shop
Safe as his scissors bathed in ultraviolet light
Obvious as spray-on hair thickener
Sharp as a cut-throat stropped on the palm

Like the brand fidelity of thieves
Discreet as the ears of a vole
Like a fluffy cocktail when you're really thirsty
Tangy as an old five-volt battery

If you can imagine a cross between
a tattoo soup and a musical sloth
or something like a cubist's routing tools
but more so, as if it had limped from the dreams
of a Gaudi of debt restructuring
or Melbourne's answer to Sydney's answer

Like the soft armchairs in funeral parlours
About as diplomatic as a wildcat
Like a traffic jam of driverless vehicles
Emphatic as the plumicorns of an owl

Frangible as a grain of incense on the anvil
Black as a drum of quenching water
Vast as the hindquarters of a rearing draught horse
Precious as a stardrop of solder

As sharp as tangy as emphatic etc.
as a trap for the only thing that will not spring it
set and tense with expectation
like a single ear of wheat in a limitless plain

Chris Andrews
from *Cut Lunch* (2002)

Marijuana Gave Me Up the Day Denis Glover Died

Once the days were clear
Like mountains in water,
The mountains were always there
And the mountain water;

Glover

I was at a party in a student flat
floorboards missing in the kitchen
vomit on the beanbag in the lounge
guy with a lampshade on his head

I suddenly knew that marijuana had given me up!

I thought it was because of What-Was-His-Name?
drowned in concrete in the hinterland to stop his mouth
you can trust concrete to shut a mouth I forget his name.

I threw my deal down on the kitchen table
– *Smoke it all because it's all over now!* –

I think I told the squatter's heir
that he couldn't play the hero
would have to carry spears on stage for years
I think I told his future wife that she had won
I'd done with young princes too that night
and their wives with shiny swinging hair.

Time strangely rearranged itself.
I found myself on the streets of Christchurch
dressed for Sydney I'd forgot it wasn't Sydney.

Reinventing a bad dream. Empty echoing streets.
With mist. Cold enough to stop your heart.
Streets went on forever both ways no traffic and no people.
I'd forgotten. This was the city that could freeze your heart.

I clung to a lamp post and laughed.
The cold had made me stupid in my head.
– *Me die? How ridiculous!* –

Woke up mysteriously in my own bed sun shining on my glory
box of wool
cast on the basque of a jersey for nobody in Tirnbertops and
Rimple bouclé
sure enough he hallooed from out on the gravel drive by the
tormented willow
– *Denis Glover's dead!* –

I call the jersey – *This One's For Denis*.
It keeps me warm but is somewhat hard to get on over my head.

My sister was a nurse in Wigton Hospital and Denis Glover died
on her ward. But she was off duty when he did.

It was the vodka did him in. And the cold.

Jennifer Compton
from *Blue* (2000)

11

The Sail and the Gannet

A single sail,
Translucent apricot,
Drifts like a poppy's petal on a frail
Breeze that is not –

A baby's breath
Of air sparingly strewn
And eked out by the estuary's width
All afternoon.

Lit from behind,
That fabric puts on show
What all of this, when the sun has declined,
Will undergo,

When like a dye
Extravagantly loosed
Late saffron through blue river and blue sky
Will be suffused.

Hours that require
Only themselves. Suspended,
Division and the eye dissolve, desire
Almost is mended.

The close of day
Approaches: echelons
Of shade and light ascend the river, grey
And flooded bronze.

That sail's no more.
And out of nowhere looms
One gannet, sweeping up and down the shore,
In the gold glooms

Seeking the day's
Last fish. So swift it flies
And circles and returns, rushing to appraise
What underlies

Its beat, it brings
A darker note into
The scene, as though to match the darkenings
That drain the view.

Too fast its flight
(And slightly desperate
Before the urgings of the loss of light)
To concentrate

Its faculties
On fish, it can't be seeing,
You feel – or it's this shadowing it sees,
And is now fleeing.

Stephen Edgar
from *Where the Trees Were* (1999)

Revisiting Coventry in Spring

You and I have lived here in the same place – our days.
And on days such as these you'd easily think you're free,
All this blue stooping, unbidden to feed from your hand,
All this green stuff – life – insouciant as a model swishing
Her skirt past your nose. How terrible, you think,
Not to know this. But even on days like these
There is another weather, life under another government.

Those wraiths of boys cruising a shopping mall
With their shark's dull hunger, the aboriginal kid sniffing
Himself dreamless, even the redundant grimly feeding
The pokies, know how they live in the same space,
The same cell as the prisoner.

Even on days like these the world is a photograph taken
Of somewhere when you weren't there. Yes: a refrigerator purrs,
Chooks fuss in a neighbouring yard, a back door closes,
The rolling boulders of traffic down in the town. And yet,
Everywhere, abstract as a town planner's map.
Even the trees brushing the window
Are just sticks in a thicket.

What you do know is the prison inside your chest
Which no space can free, which the heart beats
Its small fist against.
All who grieve know this: how each breath
Hopes that sharp, sweet air, like morphine, will this time
Bring deep draughts of relief.
Here the will is useless: limp as a flaccid penis.

This, the bare rock of exile, stripped of purpose,
Is where you are. The living think this is death,
It isn't. The dying pass through, journeying on,
But the feared gaoler, kind with unconditional acceptance,
Is with you always: should you sleep, when you wake.

Should you be released you may find warmth, sex,
A love even, but from where you have been,
Even on days like these, like an addict, a sailor
Who feels the pull of the long rolling sea
You know you've known the pure thing.
There are no terrors anywhere: you are free.

Russell Erwin
from *From Here* (2001)

Cakes

for my mother

In those far-off Empire days
when half the world was coloured pink
and life ran slow as treacle
from a spoon, the women here
were making cakes – creaming,
beating, sifting, folding,
kneeling down to yawning ovens,
with offerings of love, of obligation.

Plain cakes were for morning tea
with cinnamon and butter,
sultana ones for lunch;
chocolate, orange, lemon treats
with coconut, with cream,
for afternoons – for cricket teas,
tennis parties, bridge and euchre drives,
reaching heights of macaroon, meringue and choux
for supper guests at ten.
Serious cakes of fruit and marzipan
observed our rites of passage;
funerals, calling on reserves of taste,
decreed the classic rich madeira,
fine yet unadorned, ready
to face judgement.

The women spoke a language then
of sponges blown away,
of neenish tarts, napoleons,
butterflies and jubilees, rainbow,
devil's food, Armenian nut.
They spoke of demerara, cochineal,
angelica and silver dragees,
shapely words like talismans
to unexplored lands.

You spoke this language too,
bequeathing it to me
and though we may have laughed,
that culture born of baking
enfolded me as you,
for whenever women look
to writing in ancestral hands
this language will remain,
stained in places where the page
was splattered from the mixing bowl.

Barbara Fisher
from *Archival Footwork* (2001)

The Present Frame of the World

The present frame of the world is crumbling –
we sell ourselves for gloss, we try

so hard to glaze it; meticulously, we gild
the saints processing on its cedar lengths,

lifting it closer to art than the clutter
it contains. Who could have painted this tumble,

this sweep? Standing back, I cast about for signature
in its billowing wind of form

and colour. Towards its edges, bodies
whirl and crane: some clutch at the oiled centre,

while others are wrung, they look
to the frame and seem to see beyond it

a kind of peace. At the protected heart,
though, light fattens. Here, other bodies

are clothed in a skin that's scrubbed,
featureless. A man leans on his arm and smooths

the grass, his penis curls like a shell
on the white shore of his thigh, while women

wade in his gaze and nestle
on pillows of air. Here, rich servings of the earth

are handed about. But a face on occasion
twists and shivers, as if a whisper has drifted

through the lace afternoon, as if it has settled
on the bed of this world. As if it is known

that the frame of the world is riddled
and dry, that beyond it the galaxies turn.

John Foulcher
from *Convertible* (2000)

Her Comment

So lover,
hard shover,
hot mover,
however
half-dressed,
sweat-bathed,
how you mouthed,
how you writhed,
how you breathed
and tumesced,
with body
unsteady,
(this lady
a study
of tact,)
now lazy,
now drowsy,
it's easy
to dizzy
the fact
all your noise
brought the ease
and the ooze
of your joys
too soon,
and never,
my clever,
did lever
me over
the moon.

Alan Gould
from *Dalliance & Scorn* (1999)

Once

Shot like an arrow
through quivering distance –
not caring for the target – simply
glad to be released
from the tense, drawn bow
of one moment and the next; we are making our journey...

At first, crossing the border, an afternoon of glassy heat,
of stickily-gripping tyres
hurrying beneath
over smooth, flickering miles...

The sealed concrete highway is flecked with tiny crystals,
like the twinkling pins-and-needles
in boot-bound, swollen feet.
Curling in my socks, my numb toes uproot
themselves and wrestle into knots.

The treadmill of whirring wheels is stirring me to sleep,
but slowly. It might be hours...
the lifetime of a peach
sucked to a small stone,
another service station with old dismantled wrecks –
one, a fatal crash, with mushrooms through the seat
and a directory on the dash
('That tree wasn't on the map');
pages of other maps
like lines branching on a palm
that could have brought them anywhere,
but brought them here, thirty miles from the next town.

Until then, an autumn-coloured plain persists –
pools of water blistering the land,
crows nourishing themselves
on a meal of lard and muscle,
uncovered, wind-picked roots
clutching at dry sand.

And then, the end of endlessness… We are pulled on by the future
like a loose thread,
and the fabric of the scene is coming unstitched;
gradually, continually
unravelling as we speed
from that country dry as a cricket pitch,
into a green outfield of leisurely existence,
new landscapes being stitched
out of the old, fields of produce rolled and unrolled
as we pass the dropped stitch –
an abandoned Catholic church in an empty field.
Once, like this windshield
where rays of sunlight meet, it was the centre of all this distance.

Stephen McInerney
from *In Your Absence* (2002)

Thinking in Chunks

Chess grandmasters beat machines: they chunk
Their thoughts in patterned strategies. The flank
Attacked at Austerlitz, a hilltop link
To feints at Ulm and infantrymen bank
Around. Corporals also, other ranks when drunk
May plan from heights like this, but shrink
Back sober into line. Loose ideas junk
Like jigsaw pieces, pawns, odd lead soldiers, sink
As scuffed survivors in a nursery trunk:
Where anyone might stoop, stare down and think.

Rory Steele
from *Obverse & Parallel Lines* (2004)

Dog

I walk my dog in the wind,
he clears the grass in great leaps.
The air pushes us. He still jumps
tufts and clumps, turns, thrusts his nose,
dashes off. A hilltop, flat grass:
the wind would flatten us
but there are trees below. We hide.
The tree trunks groan and writhe:
twigs, splinters, everything loose
the wind destroys. Underneath
in the shadows, wrapped in noise,
we wait. The dog stays at my side.

Leon Trainor
from *Free Song* (1999)

Positive Psychiatry

Hearing with empathy
my tale of psychiatrist rape
and not diagnosing me as delusional...

Attending my book launch
and lining up to request
my autograph...

Offering to lend me
his copy of Wounded Healers
acknowledging my professional self...

Recognising my need for sorrow,
seeing tears as the seeds
for healing words...

Sharing her family sniffles,
strengthening my faith
in my own humanity...

Letting compassion
clearly shine
in her eyes...

Allowing me to choose
what to reveal of
my previous history...

Working together
to fight
the tardive dyskinesia...

Linette Bone
from *Healing Tears* (2001)

Heading North

Heading north, always north,
shedding the cities for the great forests
driving by the old highway
you leave upland farms, country townships,
the past flagging you down.

At truck-stops the forests dwarf you,
rising against the sky
like primordial cycads
as you splash through mountain streams
where the sun sets early

or never penetrates.
Sometimes you follow the railway track
with its glimpses of timber towns,
half-sawn tree trunks, abandoned machinery,
lighted windows after dark,

in the wake of the train whistle
a curlew's plaintive cry.
Sometimes you camp in rainforest clearings
beyond winding roads and paddocks,
gates shuttered by brambles,

listening to the sound of the forests,
ritual flight of cockatoos at morning,
the pistol-whip of birdsong.
Homeless everywhere,
you are at home here.

Margaret Bradstock
from *Coast* (2005)

Poetry Reading, Balmain

In the autumn of paintings, books
and long-lived chairs
two lines delicately map the veins
of a trembling leaf;
the voice lifts, lingers along syllables,
falls away.
The next voice tenses,
stutters commas in edgy haste,
tracking the secrets of the galaxies.

Love idles, unaware
how close to betrayal;
lust hangs heavy, finds
only the pale virtue
of a Raphael face
to feed upon.

Printed pages circulate
words gutsy as blue-veined cheese,
mellow as wine in a shaft of sun,
ambiguous as the taste of olives.

The senses coalesce.
Words weave about the curtains,
plunge from the ceiling
and phrases, velvet smooth,
cushion jagged truths.

Dinner, after such surfeit,
may be too much.

Kath Broughton
from *The Ambiguity of Olives* (2005)

You

Looking back
through the stained-glass
window of memory,
you are rounded and warm,
all knowing, loving and giving,
my very own.

Looking back
through the clear glass
window of therapy,
you are angles, sudden uplift
of thin lips
slitting
to hiss, to slide out
words directed to stab
into my heart.

Looking back
through sepia prints
you soften
        grow human,
lines crinkle around your eyes,
confuse me...
are they smiling lines
or peering lines?
Your hands droop,
clasp, stay together
on your lap...
are they two grey doves nesting
or a fist waiting to pound?

I hurry on
and through the years
race down roads, turn corners,
climb hills, pant on summits,
pause briefly in a dark wood

and one calm day
I pass a shop window,
see you
look out of my face,
see you
in every line and curve
of my body,
see you
in the colour and texture
of my coat
and come at last
to understand.

Dawn Bruce
from *Tangible Shadows* (2005)

Ode to Breakwalls

Breakwalls are like an upturned middle digit
against nature, fixed prisms surfers crave.
On common water they jostle and fidget
before tacking into waves, seeking caves.
Refraction of the swell is the attraction.
The surfboard riders voice their predilection
as the inside low tide hang glide section
barrels, before the next set provides action.

These locked rocks, this compacted cereal.
Man made refractor of the ethereal,
warping waves collapsing on flanks of banks.
Surfers paddle out as their local cranks
while off the breakwall fishermen angle
observing the scene as their lines dangle.

Michael Byrne
from *Southbound* (2005)

The Poetics of Surfing

At the Scott's Head colloquy of 1969,
proceedings began with the lighting,
by the Californians, of a ceremonial bong
with a crater like a Mexican volcano.
The first American to the rostrum
was Quentin Brown the Third, renunciate heir
to a real estate empire, who spoke prayerfully
of merging with the surge of creation
and defined the perfect wave
as the mighty utterance of the great 'Om!'

Waster Watson, the local champion,
rose to rebut and said that, for him,
the Pacific was the start of something,
not the finish, and he was going to take those sets
by the scruff of the neck and give them a caning.

And they argued on till plover-screech,
finally agreeing to two propositions:
You can't put an old Restoration hairdo
on young shoulders
and the grass is always cleaner and cheaper
from a little farm near Mullimbimby.

John Carey
from *Sorting Through Wardrobes* (2004)

Offshore Breeze

Many summers ago
on a scallop of sand edging
the bay a mother nursed her baby
under a striped umbrella

a girl gathered shells
to hear the sea's breath
a father swam where the water
was deep dark blue

and a boy lolled in green shallows
on the blown-up tube of a truck tyre
the rubber smell dissolving
into memory

Waves frisked
the black ring shorewards
white legs splayed
in homage to the sun

Suddenly the breeze turned
launching the boy on his cushioned ride
out beyond the father's stretch
out towards the deep sea channel

Mother and girl screamed
the baby squalled in a squabble of gulls
the father began his anxious trek
around the bay

        returning hours later
unshaven like a shipwrecked sailor
tube around his neck   footprints slurred
the boy asleep in his arms

Jennifer Chrystie
from *Polishing the Silver* (2006)

The Stab Pass

This was no archaic punt,
Galumphing through the wind
With that comical, sideways gait
And corkscrewing out of sight
A mile between cause and effect.

This was perfection.
The fusing of body and mind above the ball.

The mini explosion
As boot, leather and turf met
In a second of passion.

There was no colluding with the wind.
This was magic
Performed on the knife-edge.
The held breath of the crowd

And then (you hoped)
The centre half-forward marking on his chest
And turning to kick for goal.

But it's gone now,
Replaced by the university tested,
Hybridised –
Drop punt.

One does not even mention its name.

Yet, of that era, one relic remains.
The lumbering 'torp',
Catapulted for goal, now and then,
When the wind is right.

William Cotter
from *Cloud Gazing* (2005)

Honeysuckle Lane

in memory of my father

out the gate
into the back lane –
morning glory
dyed with Sydney sky,
breathing honeysuckle

long ago
you sang me its name –
when I dream
'I'll be seeing you'
in Honeysuckle Lane

growing up
has taken all my life
and many songs –
'when will you be mine,
my honeysuckle rose'

why accept
flowers faintly perfumed –
my senses
yearn to swim again
in honeysuckle

Amelia Fielden
from *Short Songs* (2003)

Keeping Up Standards

Outside her window,
the groundsman drops the barrier
to the visitors' car park,
the signal for Isobel to start
fussing with her appearance.
She rarely has visitors now,
but a lady always
makes herself presentable
in the afternoons.

With no one left to make the
journey out to the nursing home,
she is not discouraged
by her isolation.
With a steely resolve
honed by lifelong self discipline,
she has made visiting hours
the prime time of her day.

Supported, ramrod straight,
by a plinth of pillows,
hands folded on the floral doona,
she keenly observes
the outside world clattering
up and down the corridor.

A lady from the church
brings home-made sweets.
'You look nice today,
Miss Dale,' she says kindly,
and Isobel, glowing inside
with discreet pleasure,
acknowledges the compliment.

Mr Poole from upstairs
sidles into her room
to steal the piece of biscuit
left from afternoon tea,
doffing an imaginary hat
to divert her attention

'You're looking well, Isobel.
I reckon you must have a
fella tucked away in here.'
She holds back the sharp retort
that the pest is expecting,
and he retreats, defeated by
her awesome presence.

Eyes closed, she dreams again
of the promised life
wasted by a distant war.
Her chaste heart, grieving still,
catches her unawares,
sliding into numbing depths
of unresolved emotion,
the private cross
she bears with stoicism.

At five o'clock she is taken
to the bathroom in the chair
with the squeaking wheel,
deliberately chosen
by the sullen girl who calls her
Lady Muck behind her back.
As they pass by other doors,
Isobel smiles and nods,
regardless of the indifference,
secure in the knowledge that
manners are still the backbone
of a civilised existence.

Cynthia Hallam
from *Bread & Butter People* (2003)

For Joseph

Your ears will never hear sounds
that to me are ordinary as air.

From the hour that you were born
the tight white shell of silence
closed around you.
You edged away from friendship.

Silence clung and stung like sand,
smothering words before they could
break free.

Sand has a brittle sound
as it stutters underfoot.

But you are no longer like sand.
Though your ears will still never hear,
words gather, demanding as seagulls.

Now, you stretch wings towards the sky.
Glide closer to other lives.
Reach them with the rising tide
of your imperfect speech.

Dale Harcombe
from *Kaleidoscope* (2005)

Bali

In this heat
breathing is a challenge.
Walking's almost stationary.

At the hotel, breezeways with no breeze
connect sanctuaries of air conditioning.

Rice terraces: green stairs
tended by pliant people.
The hospital: and outside,
rows of dead lie neatly, shawled in white.
The guide touches my arm, his hand velvet-soft.
How old? he says. My age amazes – he laughs.
If I were Balinese, I would be dead.

We go into a small temple: lichened statues,
grey stone walls made ancient
by heat. Recent is a posy,
a supplication.
The heavy silence has a message,
but it's untranslatable, it's as though
a curtain, filmy but opaque,
hangs, infinitely enticing.

After lunch, I freeze with fever.
Hallucinate, babble. I am gomg to die, I think,
and am delighted, see myself buried beneath a tree,
covered by greenest grass, here forever,
in this most exquisite and mysterious place.

A doctor comes with unfamiliar pills.

Leaving Bali, I look out of the plane window,
see a threadlike curl of smoke, more terraces,
brown people waving, and weep,
wonder for what I am weeping.

Wonder still.

Mary Hawthorne
from *Woven All Into a Cloth* (2002)

Blood on the Moon

I am East Timorese. I am East Timorese.
                              There is blood on the moon
                              there is blood on the trees.
In the once peaceful gardens   the corpses pile high
blossom and branches are tattered and torn
                    a bloodied hair ribbon drifts in the breeze.
          I am East Timorese.
There are guns in my street
                    there are guns at my gate
Towards west of our country the death trucks are rolling.
Where is my husband   my mother   my father   my brother?
Are they gone in those trucks
              herded by strangers with guns in their hands?
Will I not ever see them again?
              I am East Timorese.
My church is in ashes, my priest is no more.
              From the bishop's last refuge flames reach to the sky
                        Did the bishop too die?
My home is on fire   my children are crying.
We must run for our lives   we have nowhere to go.
              I am East Timorese.
In Jakarta the generals are rubbing their hands
              and political puppets   from soft leather chairs
talk   unctuous as ever   and as ever
                        deceive

September 1999

Venie Holmgren
from *War & Peace* (2002)

In the House Where Keats Died

Hot and bothered, abandoning the chore
of holidays, tongues go to work
licking in water from thin streams

which jet from the Fontana della Barcaccia;
they tease the tops of gelato
while huddled in triangles of shadow

thrown out in dragon scales across
the steps of the Piazza di Spagna.
Further, at the doors of Trinita dei Monti,

the less indolent line up like footballers
mouthing the national anthem,
seeking out the dome of St Peter's

where a shining crucifix transmits
to the heavens, overseeing
the symmetry below. Too long

in the city pent, I sit in the Casina Rossa
where, consumed and broken,
Keats abandoned symmetry altogether.

And from across the sea, I too
receive the lick of love
which tangles, spoils the sonnet.

I spot prodigal clouds drifting northward.
They're avoiding that golden cross
and taking leave, as I will

from this heat and loneliness
to rejoin that congregation
cooling below in the shadows.

George Huitker
from *An Unfamiliar Actor* (2002)

Caroline – Come – Early

Not real
just a doll
why did she come so soon?
Five weeks early,
how do you handle a too-new life
that should still be in the womb?
It's inhospitable out here
without a lifeline.
So aware of her fragility
as if daring to breathe would harm her.
Only a little red face visible
between swaddling
and tiny pink and white beanie
perfect in every detail.
I want to touch
feel her warm flesh
make her real to me.
She raises hairless eyebrows!
True!
Then repeats the trick
in case I missed it the first time.
Not a doll,
a person
already asserting her own personality.

Rosemary Jaensch
from *Still Bemused* (2004)

Cool Change

Humidity stifles
heat presses down.

Motionless garden
silent the house.

Soft as a moth wing
uncertainly felt

a cool breath descends
raindrops are dealt.

Wind pushes harder
trees come alive

branches toss leaves
to spiralling rain

coaxing sweet scent
from freshening air.

Tension diminished
house timbers creak.

Clouds brush the moon
the earth breathes deep.

Angela Johnson
from *Neon Moons* (2004)

Snapshot

The old ghost
of a young girl
appeared out
of a roll of celluloid film,
developing into a beauty,
smiling
from the shade
of her wide-brimmed, plumed hat,
at the camera lens,
over a century ago,
into my eyes.

She wears a frilled white blouse,
brooched at the throat,
mutton chop sleeves
in a jacket drawn in
at a tiny eighteen-inch waist.

Behind her,
on the deck of the steamship,
black smoke fixed at the funnel,
groups of gentlemen
stand about
in top hats and bow ties.

Ladies, in long skirts
and big hats,
holding parasols,
lean on the rails.

In the distant background,
the masts of sailing ships,
and a phaeton
running along the pier.
Out of a tin trunk,
through layers of worn copies
of Dickens, faded diaries,
notebooks and ledgers,
brittle with penned ink,
and the dusty debris
of a pair of cufflinks,
some buttons,
a gold sovereign knotted
in a gold silk handkerchief,
out of a tiny, cracked film,
rose the buried ghost of a girl.

Who is she?
Not my grandmother.
A deceased great-aunt
in her youth?
A cousin recorded
in the family tree?
There is no one
from her Age to tell me
her name.
No one to identify
the girl
where beats a heart
of sentiments
unknown to me.
In a time
I cannot comprehend,
in an atmosphere
which grew the clothes
she wore,
she blossomed
into an extinct flower,
fossilised in a celluloid film.

Judith E.P. Johnson
from *Landmarks* (2005)

The company of spiders

The spider finds a home
on the kitchen window sill

suspended among glass
bottles and jars.

A mandala pregnant with meaning
she squats and waits –

her back bubbling with unborn babies.
By morning her children are leaving

the dead body and moving out
from the centre of the web

along delicate threads
to the circle's rim.

'You can't just leave them there!'
my daughter protests,

arms flailing, hands flapping;
while her brother suggests

flushing them down the sink.
As the children ready for school

I take the jar outside,
place it in the garden

amongst fallen bark and snowgrass,
and linger in the company of spiders.

Ray Liversidge
from *Obeying the Call* (2003)

Anzac Day

The agony of flowers is greatest at the cenotaph.
Poor widow, that uniform will no more fit a name
Years later, no, nor bugles ever blow
Deathless finality more than poets can, whose poor paragraph
Stirs spent guns to anger or calls sadness to attention.
But mourn now while you are in fashion
And we have time to spare for some compassion.

Only the agony of flowers seems true, lasting, appropriate.
Share it now, while rank by rank the comrades of the wars
Put learnt patience in their ceremonial tread
And kindness in a look that one time held a bayonet.
The shuffle of their footsteps passes, but while we strive to
Label pity on this box of hours,
Creation bleeds in the agony of flowers.

Ronald Liversidge
from *Collected Poems* (2005)

Dransfield: An Elegy

I don't quite remember how I came to you.
It may have been during those long train journeys,
commuting convolutedly from home to university:
my arduous punishment for flunking school.

Four days a week, for three and a half years
in a carriage filled with monastic austerity,
I tightly hugged an eclectic stack of books,
devoured them page after page for survival.

Author led indirectly to author. .
Each one became a new relationship,
a fresh intimacy between imaginations.
Then your verse filled my veins, infused my blood.

'Pas de deux for lovers', 'Loft, for Hilary',
the thoughts of a life immersed in metaphor.
Almost at once I understood exactly
your drive to coalesce with language and flesh.

But poetry lost its potency for you.
Speeding one moment, oblivion the next.
'Once you have become a drug addict,
you will never want to be anything else.'

It's decades since they put you underground.
A victim of risk-taking, chemicals and feelings.
Twenty-four years was hardly enough time
to jettison your baggage or clarify a vision.

Eight years older now than you were at death
I contemplate the waste, the fish that got away.
This poem is in honour of your courage and foolishness.
These lines belong to you the way you belong to us.

There is no other method of living in this world.
To write is to distance, to distance is to love.
At least that's the way you figured it worked.
I wrestle with such theories, today, at this moment.

Mark Mahemoff
from *Near-life Experience* (2002)

White Mecca 1975

I was thirteen and wore a bikini. I was lean then. We were all
lean. We would lean with the steep of the climb. Into the steep.
Up the slope. Into sky. I don't remember clouds. Just that glistening sand heap. The ridge of its crest, precise on Mediterranean
blue. Everything so precise. We were lean and precise. Our
muscles tingled with the climb. No dune grass then. No spinifex
to grasp. No grass to grip. Only white and blue before us. Grains
of glass glittering in sand. We were cool in dark glasses. Shaz,
Carlos and Dazza; the kid they called Fat Albert, and me. All lean,
except Albert who would puff up the dune red-faced, dripping
sweat, like a pork roast oozing dripping. The only one in jeans.
Fat Albert – we all forgot his real name. He never swam. The slide
down dunes was his ultimate thrill. We cheered him on. Always
the fastest. Shifting his weight for the slide, he excelled. Dragging
himself out of the river like a wet blimp. We walked barefoot
from Christies to Port Noarlunga. No fear of needles. Along the
Esplanade. Up and over the bluff. Bypassing the jetty. We sought
our white Mecca. Our ecstasy. Our ascension. The struggle of
climbing. The thrill of the ride. All the way. Over the edge. The
cool of the river. Its bed of thick mud swallowed more than our
ankles, even then. We joked about bodies of dead cats – growling
ghosts – deep down in the suck of mud. We felt their rough
tongues on the soles of our feet. Clambered out quickly to the
sanctuary of white. We stopped at the kiosk to buy orange
frosties. Strip off the sticky paper. Cool our tongues on coloured
ice. Remembering how, in winter, the river would rise above its
banks and flood the kiosk. Its cool concrete floor – a balm for
burning feet. There were always sandbags stacked outside. The
heat was our god though. The sun. Our summer lifestyle. Hor-
mones. Pulsing in speedos. Our lean teen summer. Whole days
climbing that sand dune. As our sun-god travelled across the sky.
Aching for water. From the kiosk, we trekked along the dunes, in
the rush of voices – the laughing, the squealing. Someone would

bring a sheet of masonite, or an old tin signboard, salvaged from a vacant block of land. (We'd brush the snail crust off the tin and use it to slide on.) We climbed the steep white into sky. Again and again. Almost breathless. We were soft shift in glistening sand. We queued at the crest of white on blue – like a wave of sand – gathering to break over the wetlands, the estuary. Gazing out across the river, the road-bridge, as cars silently ascended and descended the grey bitumen strip of Norwood Hill. Finally, we grasped the edge of the sun-hot sheet and blessed it like a prayer mat. Shifting our weight for the adrenalin slide. Gasping in the air rush, amid the cheering. Down the pristine slope. Sometimes, all the way to the river. Into the splash of dubious water. The shocking cool. The ghosts of dead cats licking our heels.

Deb Matthews-Zott
from *Shadow Selves* (2003)

Imagination

There is no shape, no closing wall,
no boundary fence to ride.
Its kingdom is that other world
where Gods are said to stride.

A fabled place of magic sails
that release our earthly tie,
and lift us high above the clouds
where we begin to fly.

Oh, flights of fearless fancy!
Such wondrous, soaring things.
How sweet it is to drift aloft
on a dreaming beat of wings!

To step inside a moment
that resonates with blue,
and there beside the endless sky,
come face to face with you.

The image of perfection;
the beauty of your birth.
To catch a glimpse of paradise,
before falling back to earth.

Ian McFarlane
from *Evening at Murunna Point* (2001)

Manic Mary

'Good morning, Mary, I'm...'

'Yes' she said 'I'm Mary. Mary, that's me! Mary me, marry me! Bet you can't carry me! Ha ha! You can't make me or break me or dictate to me. Dictators!'

'Mary...'

'Don't get violent with me, young man! Where did you get those spectacles? Take them off. Take them off! Don't get violent, get eloquent. Grandiloquent! Like me! Ha ha!'

'M...'

'M-m-m-Mary, quite contrary, ha ha! Doctor, locked her, locked her up! For half a buck. Half her luck... Doctor what are you doing? Doktor? Doktor Foktor went to Glockter in a paddle of pain. If we don't wheedle, he won't wield the needle. Doing what? Doing what? Doctor?...'

Tim Metcalf
from *Cut to the Word* (2002)

Looking in on Wallace Stevens

You have to read him
to see in such clear air
your real self
as you have always been –

At the foot of these wide stone steps,
looking straight to camera
with a sternness fading
from claims, indemnities,

Decisions calmly taken –
maybe a size too large for life
in your easily fitting
favourite pale grey suit,

One wisp of your hair out of place.

John Miles
from *A Writing Unexpected* (2002)

Playground

Against the fence
he stands as straight
as the knife-sharp

creases defining
steel-grey suit pants
one continuous plumbline

of back, pole and suit
as though being vertical
is the only defence

the only protection
against the fluid
lines of life

the old man
drunk on the bench
the casual curling

of lovers passing by
and the terrifying swing
the pendulum curves

of his children flying
precariously free
against his life's gravity.

Ann Nadge
from *Fence Music* (2004)

Girl on a Swing

A hot sticky
Southern summer day
She sat
Barefoot
Dressed in hand-me-downs

Swinging her legs
Back and forth
Scuffing the dust
Beneath her feet

Smiling
She gazed upwards

I saw nothing
To smile about
No toys, no bicycle
Nothing

I settled a chair beside her
Aligned my gaze to hers,

Gradually I saw
A colour, gently flapping,
And the lightness of
Butterfly flight

And found
I, too, was smiling

Barbara Olds
from *Boundary Rider* (2003)

A Very Short Woman Flies To Perth

She was worrying walking over the tarmac
this plane is so small
metal shimmered, overtaking her thoughts
she clanged up the plane steps her travel bag flapping
and beating itself on her legs
it's so small this plane she muttered
her mantra of pleading, a wide-bodied jet
a wide-bodied jet,
crew were smiling and taking her arm and her bag
overhead lockers always so small
she grew paler and paler in her seat full of silence
she imagined herself falling her bag falling
her size six dress and her child sized shoes
falling and falling
the noise of the engines stopped all her thoughts
there was no turning back
she flattened the tray's beige horizon
against the din of the engines, she hated the sound
her feet dangled for three and a half hours.

Christine Paice

from *Mad Oaks* (2003)

Free

Oysters wrap their hurt in pearl,
whales make love
between sheets of liquid silk
the early full moon sheds its mask
into the ocean.

Ioana Petrescu
from *Fumigated* (2001)

Socialist with a Human Face

From appearances in tributes
he is a weather-hardened bosun
whose books were his compass,
whose articles of resistance
created charts for others to follow.

His marching understanding
with those who enjoyed
the devil in his humour,
forged friendships
as nurturing as his romance with Shelley.

As unencumbered by possessions
as wild geese flying south for winter,
he inspired those who watched
by staying airborne
towards only one destination.

He found the winds to blow
over the sludge of hypocrisy,
his words flowed unstoppable
towards ideals that anyone might ride
the motion from his waves.

He was against the violence of conquerors,
he saw as no better than spivs
those who posed in politics
or sold phoney products
even from judges' benches.

He was for the disadvantaged,
the hair shirts of conscience
and the stifled
who needed his replies
as evidence of their innocence.

Never an optional extra,
his radicalism was the bloodstream,
his self mockery an abiding badge
even for the crutches
of his final years.

(Tribute to journalist Paul Foot, 1937–2004)

Stuart Rees
from *Tell Me the Truth About War* (2004)

Summer In Hobart

Summer at last. The yellow air
is heady with privet blossom,
stone fruits swell and soften,
a light breeze lifts the scent
from lavender and rose.

The river's a silk scarf, sequined
with lights, patterned with wings.
Hills on the far shore glow, sunning
golden haunches. Further distant,
smudged blue ranges, the milky sky.

My garden dreams in the sun, filled
with a ceaseless conversation:
cricket's sharp tintinnabulation,
crow's harsh croak, wren chatter.
In my neighbour's yard a wind chime plays.

The hammering street noise fades.
Mind's clamour, daily traffic, now subsides
as ear attunes to subtle orchestrations
of light and air. This moment's measure
overflows.

Lyn Reeves
from *Speaking with Ghosts* (2002)

A Butterfly

The child is father of the man. – Wordsworth

This hot sun has made the garden thirsty;
I stand and hose, and push the dog's muzzle
from the nozzle.

The girl child next door climbs the back fence
to say hello; her radiance
lights the greenery.

Our dog runs to reach up and love her too.
'Look,' she says, 'under this leaf. A black butterfly.'
We greet it too,

so recently a chrysalis. 'Underneath,'
she guides us, 'it has lovely colours' –
to our surprise.

My wife's smile and Emma's are equally
beautiful. They correspond, each on
the cusp of something:

Emma – it will be puberty.
This child will be mother surely
of the woman.

Marilyn – a new phase of living,
richly in the present. I see how much
both are giving.

They share the butterfly as a mutual gift.
I see them: woman on the dappled path,
smiling up,

child above, supported by the fence,
smiling through the greenery,
the dog reaching up

whimpering with keenness to touch
and be touched. The butterfly enjoys
a brief flowering.

Max Richards
from *Catch of the Day* (2006)

Haiku

their earthly lives pass
memories stay treasured
faithful dogs ever

wind scatters spirit
lightly with grey driven rain
heaven vaults over

camellia drops
flower season in pass time
pale petals on grass

Alice Shore
from *Birds Dare Not Whisper* (2005)

Things he has stolen

Forbidden fruit from an orchard
not knowing about expulsion.
Shoes from a shop, comics, bicycle parts
his disdain for adornment, popular
literature, & speed, undeveloped.
Groceries, cigarettes from cars
well, basics are important.
Till money from a stingy employer
militant action he does not regret.
The Popemobile, a fraught joyride
but it was only a whisky dream.
Milk, newspapers, a fresh start
needs of first light's exposure.
Hearts, hope, trust (not taken lightly)
the fewer words about shame the better.
A barking dog from next-door neighbours
black & white, the mutt, not the story.
extra Britrail travel, one wheelie bin
but no partridge in a pear tree.
Coins from an electricity meter
thin times, desperate measures.
Income tax & sexual technique
own up, he is not alone.
Jokes, magic, artful gestures, words
ditto the third last line.

Ian C. Smith
from *This Is Serious* (2003)

Ballad of a chopped-up house

(with apologies to Philip Larkin and A.A. Milne)

I am a room in a chopped-up house
(in a five-bed, no-lounge, chopped-up house)
and there once was a lady lived in me
was as far round the bend as she could be –
but was fine, far as anyone else could see –
in a chopped-up house in Cambridge.

She dragged every day to her fucked-up job
and she moaned home again from her fucked-up job.
She peeled off her days like sweat-soaked clothes
and she piled them in corners and piled them in rows –
unwashed, unexamined, and on the nose,
in a chopped-up house in Cambridge.

Bits of meals she dredged from the cramped-up stove;
and the grease-caked pots from the cramped-up stove;
and last month's news, and the month's before;
all mulching down on my mouldering floor,
with her piled days pushing against the door
of her locked-up room in Cambridge.

Still she shoved through my knee-deep, choked-up space –
through her days, unreclaimed, in my choked–up space.
Her bed was a pile of unopened mail
and her dreams were of soapies, and telesales,
and a dim understanding going stale
in a chopped-up house in Cambridge.

And then one day, in the chopped-up house,
she stopped dragging out to her fucked-up job.
The house-mates thought it was slightly queer
but did nothing (discreetly) for over a year –
not till the rot-stench and rats appeared
in the chopped-up house in Cambridge.

When the landlord forced through my locked-up door
she was festering there on my fouled-up floor:
dwarfed by her heaped-up life's debris;
overcome by the fumes of her lethargy.
She'd been fine – far as anyone else could see –
in a chopped-up house in Cambridge.

Melinda Smith

from *Pushing thirty, wearing seventeen* (2001)

Darling Di

I can see her in a French farce –
the ageing wanton,
flashing pantaloons,
grinning lewdly.
Slash of red, missing her mouth.
Rouged dots on the cheeks.
Nipples too – she shrieks.

Mammon's ancient goddess,
flaunting, flashing.
Gold and glitter –
shimmering, seducing.
Every day a carnival –
gaudy trinkets, leering smiles.
Lots of money, lots of toys.
Endless fun, endless chatter.

Spinning, spinning.
The giddy refrain bleating on.
Me, me, fun, fun, buy, buy.
Head full of fluff –
expensive fluff.
Bought it at Georges.
Better than a brain.
Didn't you know,
they're not in, this season, darling!

Karen Throssell
from *The Old King* (2003)

See to Believe

You would not believe what I have seen.

I have seen cloud weighty as lead
Crouching lion on the rim of the Brindabellas
Full of impending winter.
I have seen a baby covered in blood and blinking, his cord uncut
From me; I kissed him bloodied and crying, an angel.
I have seen rosebuds filled with dewdrops
Opening slowly into spring sun.
I have seen children laughing and rolling in dirt.
I have seen my grandfather just before death, cry out to God.
I have seen my grandmother weeping for babies unborn.
I have seen statesmen lying, baldfaced, before millions,
And ordering youth to war for money,
For power.
Is this ignorance or evil? It has happened before.
I have seen a man broken by weakness and anger
Self-destruct and fall away.
I have seen truth unspoken in a look.
I have seen the sun rise as though it were the first day
A slow colouring of the world, a dawning,
A rising of bloodorange light, and all birds and dogs
Heralding the mystery of light with flapping and rattling
And joyous warbling and the rough bark and pant.

I have seen my children sleeping, with breath light and
Rhythmic, skin unimpeachable, foreheads uncreased,
Trusting me and the world in their deeply peaceful unconsciousness.
I have felt their hands upon my face and lips in
Mornings of sleepy warm joy,
That sprang from me, and from eternity, to warm me there
And fill my sleepy heart with gratitude.

I have seen mountains.
I have seen the sea,
And the sky like a vertiginous ocean above;
Completely new creatures, places, cultures, unearthed from the
Glorious Mystery of the world, discovered when all was thought to be
    known;
Headlines, amazement, when that which has always been known since
The dawn of time to be true, is proved –
The inhumanity of battle, the necessity of love, the evil of greed, the sanctity
    of life.
I have seen people sharing the last of their food.
I have seen people giving blood.
I have seen violence.
I have seen hate bloom like algae, watered by toxic tears of loss.
I have seen a million perfect things placed within our reach-
The perfect sustenance of bread, the light like honey, the water Divine.
Each of the millions its own small miracle.
To think that a moment of passionate chaos may bring forth life...
Or witness sheer strangenesses– chameleon, platypus, armadillo-
The magnitude of a tiger's symmetry, or dawning day, or stars.

I am mute with wonder
At all I have seen, and not,
That there is more to see
Than can ever be seen,
That these truths may be overlooked in a careless blindness,
Or worse, that they may be perceived and renounced;
That that which is known must
Eternally be learnt over.

Sarah Tiffen
from *Learning Country* (2005)

midnight swim

(for a woman taken by a crocodile while swimming in Hartley's Creek, North Queensland)

canned laughter echoes
round the mangrove stilts
in a Cairns backwater. humidity cleaves
like armour plating, night stretches,
a patient beast content with watching,
  and you slide into the shallows,
the silk of scarcely wrinkled water

garden lights ebb and now on the surface,
water against skin, and you can't help yourself
  in this seductive wet –
musie or lust electrifies the night,
and your face bobs on the water
like a lantern. did you forget

the softness of bodies out of their element
what you knew in daylight –
  that log poking slowly
against the current?
  you weren't a water lily
or a frog, improbably green,
clinging to a gaping jaw

you knew the reptilian economy –
sun-soaked days, nights of arousal –
you'd heard them roaring each to each
  in the swamps at night

afterwards, the hunters of the district
        shot up everything in sight,
hungry for a body, a perpetrator.
searching entrails for a sign,
        they found a fingernail.
it's not a matter of reprisals
(those inner lids close and close again
        like the doors of alien spacecraft)

out of your territory without a weapon,
your arms lifting the weight
and coolness of water,
you gave the signal for the strike,
death-rolled into silence

Louise Wakeling
from *Medium Security* (2002)

the drowning

Aunt Lily taught me how
to drown kittens

you can do this
she said
girls of nine
are not yet
emotionally aware
you won't mind

see   you hold them down
in the bucket
they will struggle
they will cry
don't look so scared
take care   they'll scratch
don't let them up

push your fingers hard
on each head
spread your hands
like this   look

they can't live   can't live here

I'll wait inside
it might take a while

when it's done
I'll help you
wrap them for the bin

Aunt Lily said   it's such a shame
you're trembling dear   you can't cry now
it's no one's fault   you must be strong

when they're quiet
knock on the door   and I'll make tea

let's see how grown-up you can be

Irene Wilkie
from *Love & Galactic Spiders* (2005)

Ode To My Squatter's Chair

(With thanks to W.H. Davies)

'What is this life if, full of care,
we have no time to stand and stare?'

No time now that I'm sixty-five
to celebrate I'm still alive?

No time to sprawl in my squatter's chair,
head laid back, feet in the air?

No time to lounge on the back veranda
And let my thoughts compose and wander?

No time to gaze across the plot
and absorb the beauty of this spot?

No time to relax without a care
and nose the heavily-scented air?

No time to marvel how galahs are able
to feed to the rhythm of the swinging bird table?

No time to relish the cooling breeze
and listen to lorikeets in the high trees?

No time to watch the darkening sky
and the gathering stormclouds rolling by?

No time to wonder what's the matter
with the kookaburras with their raucous chatter?

No time to unwind when day is done
and follow the slowly-setting sun?

No time just to sit and drift and doze
and savour my retirement years' repose?

A poor life this if, full of care,
I can't enjoy my squatter's chair.

Ray Wilson
from *Resurrection* (2004)

Short History of the Twentieth Century

Main Street cinema Indians were routed nightly to cheers
And, on a sudden, the jerky comical uniforms started bleeding

Mad Nietzsche, blind Kipling, crippled little Henley
Still coaxed sparks from grovelling recruits

Grenades tied to the ears of black, brown and yellow
Without remorse and sermons to their orphans too

The great voice was the megaphone and wireless relays
Fresh-lysoled peasants dinned with calculated hate

To be an intellectual and kill was the new fashion
And communiqués ceased announcing children as casualties

As madness left the survivors in a long sick weariness
The oppressed were caught in a bewildered frenzy

All's eaten up as weevils and locusts do,
Our Darwinian favourites – Nature powders to metallic dust

Rush to the seas and industrial vomit laps you.
Starved heads protrude from heaps of guarded grain

White coats, personable as angels
Tinker with germs and hand them to the village idiot

The mechanical and imbecilic moon is re-cosseted for advice,
Tooth-fairy philosophies, scrabble on a ouija board

Mere colonels with toffee teeth, fondling little girls,
Polish atomic buttons and talk of re-loving their mothers

Our air conditioning, panoramic wall paper and indoor garages
Will shield us, will save us, deliveries through the slit of a chained door

What's left but to slug your veins – the Ali punch
Leaves honourable writhing casualties merrily vaunting

This is the twentieth century, we fly our madness
And the asphalt of parking lots hides the mass graves

Julian Woods
from *Heroes of the Twentieth Century* (2001)